Dream Big
And
Act Fast

Develop the Abundance Mindset

That Leads You To

Prosperity, Growth & Wealth

Paperback ISBN: 9798388956880

© *2023 Mesiti Pty Ltd*

Compiled by Pat Mesiti, David Cavanagh & Robert Plank

DreamBigActFast.com

Dream Big
And Act Fast

Develop the Abundance Mindset That
Leads You to Prosperity, Growth and Wealth

Pat Mesiti, David Cavanagh
Graham Ropata, Martine Lambert, Julie Korte, Ian Cory
Jacqueline Day, Billie Wilde, Dr. Gerald Nyasulu, Collin Harrison

Chapter 1: Reset Your Perspective! Begin Your Journey to Help Others | Graham Ropata 1

Chapter 2: Trust The Process! Hard Work, Confidence, Gratitude & Success | Martine Lambert...................... 11

Chapter 3: Activated Living! The Secret to Your Best Quality of Life as You Age | Julie Korte..................... 27

Chapter 4: Adjust Your Sails! Grow, Scale & Thrive in Your Business | Jacqueline Day.................................... 45

Chapter 5: Work From Home! Build An Online Business To Support Your Lifestyle, Retirement & Legacy | Ian Cory 59

Chapter 6: Allow Your Dream! The Secret Formula For Body, Mind & Spiritual Success | Billie Wilde 75

Chapter 7: Knowledge! Your Spirituality, Happiness, Freedom And Success Is All About What You Know | Dr. Gerald Nyasulu 93

Chapter 8: God is Greater Than Any Man! Your Faith Can Move Mountains | Collin Harrison 113

Chapter 9: Dream Big And Take Massive Action | David Cavanagh... 127

Chapter 10: Reinvent Yourself And Act Fast | Pat Mesiti 139

Chapter 1: Reset Your Perspective! Begin Your Journey to Help Others | Graham Ropata

"A dream written down with a date becomes a goal.
A goal broken down into steps becomes a plan.
A plan backed by action makes your dreams come true."
— *Greg Reid*

Do you struggle to fit in? Where do you belong with your family and culture?

Imagine being 30 metres underwater, trying to salvage a sunken fishing boat, or riding 10 metre swells up and down rock faces picking crayfish off the rocks.

Growing up as a teenager, my lifestyle was full of adventure. I knew no other way to live. If I was not on the water, I was under it. I have seen things that most people can only watch on television.

We Came, We Saw, We Conquered, We Learned

My parents gave me away when I was three months old, and I was raised white by my grandparents. There's nothing wrong with that— they loved me, yet lacked change in a changing world.

They were old school. They did not like the Māori culture, so I missed out on a cultural experience, plus two following generations missed out.

Many times, I visited my parents and formed a good relationship, but I never fit in.

I hated school. I only attended to play rugby, played a game called fives, and sold the lunch my grandmother made. I was a budding entrepreneur. I was in need of a mentor— someone special who could see my hidden potential and, like water drawn from a well, pull it to the surface.

Walking home from school, a neighbour stopped me and asked, "What are you doing for the next four and a half years?" My quick reply, "Nothing." So, I completed an apprenticeship in carpentry. I built many nice homes.

During that time, I completed a scuba course, gained commercial skippers and engineering tickets. I started a new adventure: commercial fishing and diving.

My boat rolled over in heavy seas. My crew of one and myself abandoned the vessel, dressed in our diving gear in the water, and swam a couple of kilometres to shore. If we had missed the shoreline, the next stop was Antarctica.

We fought for our own survival. There was no time to think. Within 30 seconds, we were standing on the deck of a fishing boat, and the next moment, we were swimming. There was no time to issue a mayday call.

Our ability to perform work underwater saved our lives. We came, we saw, we conquered, we learned.

Ignited Passion

Education did nothing for me. Learning street smarts from the hard school of knocks allowed me to never fail at anything.

I have made a heap of mistakes. I came out better after learning from those mistakes. Some, I had to learn more than once.

I still did not know where I belonged. Having a wife and family to support, "working hard" was the only solution I knew.

Moving to Australia to continue fishing didn't work. When my son died, just 21 days old, it really hurt. We were in a strange country with no friends. Life sucked. I continued with fishing and drinking— we all manage pain differently.

I took a taxidermy course and mounted native animals for a local museum. That led to ten years in meat works, beginning on the kill floor, rising rapidly to a Quality Assurance Officer, and writing a Quality Assurance Manual, described as one of the best in Australia.

I did it "my way." Then one day, it happened— I collided headfirst into God. I attended church, and I instantly knew what I wanted to be: a great motivational speaker— changing lives with the spoken word.

That's what drives me— that ignited passion— birthed deep within a person believing that whatever has gone on in my life, I can help someone through their heartache and pain.

I have had the opportunity to travel around Australia and New Zealand while motivational speaking, and have witnessed many signs and wonders. One day, I said to God, "We have not raised anyone from the dead."

His quick reply, "Yes, you have. How about those in the church?"

He was referring to the Pastor, leadership, musicians, and congregation. How can God send people into the local church in such a mess? So guess who He sends?

"Many are called. Few are chosen."

Why? They choose NOT to be chosen.

I am captaining a tourist vessel part-time. I meet interesting people. Most think I am a real estate agent because of the historical properties I share with them, especially the prices they are sold for, but no one believes it.

This leads into areas of the real estate market and property development, areas I love. Many take my business card for later contact. Offers to come to stay and have a meal are expressed.

I express the same enthusiasm whether one or fifty passengers are aboard.

Desire presents an opportunity for others to accomplish their own desires.

Start Strong

When you meet someone new and interesting, and you have a chance to speak up and deliver your own personal, power message— capture their attention with a strong introduction. They can set their own boundaries regarding how this adventure will proceed.

Read their body language, make eye contact, and have fun. Research your topic. Be prepared for the questions you are not expecting.

It's like baking a cake— without all the ingredients, the cake fails.

When you share, let that God-given ability that you have been blessed with, come to the forefront. Leave nothing in your fuel tank.

If you can't do it for yourself, then do it for your family, for those less fortunate than you, homes for the homeless, or a hospital for the sick.

What turns you on? Write down your vision. Be careful about the friends you keep and the information you digest. Show me your friends, television, and social media, and I will show you your future.

Garbage in, garbage out. How about "Positive In, Positive Out?"

Influence & Perspective

Wisdom, knowledge and understanding— are all required to make this work. *Wisdom* is what's in your head. *Knowledge* is what's in your heart. *Understanding* is what comes out of your mouth.

Your dress code communicates who you are. You never get a second chance to make that first impression.

Believe in yourself, regardless of what others say. Do not set limits upon yourself. It takes focus to build precept upon precept. Be precise and clear about where you desire to end up.

When you set aside your self-ego, things will become clearer. You are the creator of all of your objections, so it is time to take responsibility for those objections.

Follow up on yourself. It does not matter if the goal you set failed. Maybe the bar you set was too high. Reset, go again. Take smaller bites.

You are your own type of stock market, so produce shares that go up in value. Help others achieve their goals, dreams, and visions.

You are where you are today by the choices that you made in your past. Start fresh. Replace the old soil, plant some new seeds, and believe in a fresh new harvest. Or stay in the same place as you are today, watch life go by, and occasionally think of what could have been.

When you acquire a perspective of what you can do in your life, you can help others.

About Graham Ropata

Graham Ropata was born in Akaroa, a small town outside of Christchurch on the South Island of New Zealand. He has no school qualifications other than he attended school, yet  went on to achieve much within the building industry continuously working for himself, worked on, and ran his own commercial fishing vessel, commercially dived for Paua (abalone) taxidermy, meat works, Pastor, tourist vessel captain, and the list continues.

What are the desires within your heart? Are you prepared to take the next step to launch yourself into the deep?

Chapter 2: Trust The Process! Hard Work, Confidence, Gratitude & Success | Martine Lambert

I was fortunate to have been born and raised in France, growing up in a small village surrounded by a loving family and a vast playground called nature. My childhood family was not wealthy in monetary terms, but we were rich. We had all the love, encouragement and support we ever needed. We never went without any of the basics, including good, healthy, locally grown food.

I was a happy child— full of life, joy, curiosity and a general zest for living. The saying, "It takes a village to raise a child" was literally true for me. People looked out for me, but I was free to explore my surroundings in safety and play outside, encompassed by the wonders of nature.

Birds fascinated me. I would spend hours watching them wheel and dive through the air with grace and beauty. I was in awe. I was encouraged to be curious and open minded. I was inspired to use and explore my active imagination. One day, my Mother told, "Martine, stop swallowing cherry pips, or one day, you will have a cherry tree growing out of your ears!" That got my imagination humming, and I decided from that day onwards I would only eat chicken wings, in the firm belief that I would grow wings and be free to fly anywhere.

Why Not Choose To Be Happy?

My Mother was one of my best teachers. She showed me how to feel comfortable with nature and with life. Often, she said, "With time, everything will work out fine." She was correct about the seeds she planted in our garden, but she had trouble understanding why her philosophy did not work with people. Why did they sometimes act so unhappy for no obvious reason? Why did friends and family destroy themselves with negative thinking? Why not choose to be happy?

Mum taught me to learn by doing. When I got something wrong, it was a learning experience. We were always busy. Today, working out how to do things is mostly easy. Mum taught me to learn life through nature. If birds and plants could figure out life, I could too.

Boarding school changed my life. I was taken from a natural instinctive lively world, deposited on what might as well have been a foreign planet. I was judged on what I could memorise, how I behaved in class, and how closely I obeyed rules. Each time I tried to act like another student or emulate a teacher, I was struggling against the natural "me" and I felt artificial.

However, I discovered that I was good at helping people who were experiencing difficulties. When I was 16, my best friend fell pregnant and did not want to tell her parents. I was committed to helping her, so I used my allowance to advance her money for an abortion, and I stayed with her until she recovered. I was unconsciously following the power within me.

Hard Work Leads To Confidence

After school, I followed the same path as most other people— working and struggling to understand why things "were not working out." Without much connection to the real me, my self-esteem plummeted.

I believed that to live the life I wanted, I needed a boost in confidence. To gain that confidence, I needed to work hard and push myself. Clawing my way to the mythical top was too high a cost for me. I moved to Australia and started again, learning the language and culture, re-building my life, being "normal."

One day, I found a trace of the original, natural me. A small voice in my mind asked some serious questions: What is life about? Am I here to work and struggle without enjoyment, just to survive?

Feeling Unworthy Of Success

I had enough of feeling stuck in most areas of my life. I caught myself thinking the worst in every situation. I lived in fear of making any decision. I was consumed by what others thought of me. I believed it was better to live life doing as others do — make everyone else feel comfortable at my expense.

I felt like a single drop of water hanging onto a cliff near the edge of the waterfall, afraid I would be swept away all alone with my fears and troubles. Nobody else could feel like I did. My emotional pain couldn't be understood by anyone else.

I surrounded myself with more "stuff" and felt better for a short time, but I found myself hating myself — because I had more of what I had learned long ago as "failure" rather than "success." Thus, I was unworthy.

Maybe I could be redeemed by making other people happy? I was a natural people pleaser, so I would do almost anything, but it was never enough. I was preyed upon by those people who seek doormats like me, and it was a long time before I reached my limit. I reached the point of burn-out. I was exhausted, depressed, and hanging on for other people's approval.

A Carrot Can't Be A Cabbage

One day, I woke up with the realisation that I knew very little about me. I remembered a saying from my childhood, "A carrot can't be a cabbage." That led me to the question: Why was I following the path that I believed society had designed for me, instead of following my unique blueprint? I was choosing this life. I desperately wanted to be a carrot, but I was actually a cabbage! No big deal, it's just a saying, right? Wrong.

This thought caused me to look around at the lost, miserable people around me who believed the same as me: we were all in the middle of a materialistic world, searching for help from someone else, believing we were beyond redemption. Other people seemed to be struggling, just like me! The individual drop of water had been resisting the waterfall because it was scary, let go, and began the journey with other like-minded drops of water to become a stream, river, ocean of individual drops of water.

A self-development course introduced me to a fresh, new way of thinking. I knew it was my future from day

16

one. I saw, in my mind's eye, that child of nature, that real "me." I had a new goal. It was up to nobody else but me to find and rescue the one person I had ignored all those years. Me! They say, "When the student is ready, the teacher will appear." I was ready.

The Most Valuable Image I Have Ever Seen

My teacher introduced me to a simple image that showed how my mind works. It remains the single most valuable image that I have ever seen. I set out on a quest to find out who Martine is. Despite setbacks, disappointments and struggles, I kept at it. I finally found where confidence comes from. I realised I did not have to claw my way over opponents or colleagues to get to the mythical "top."

This is true for you, too. You need nothing more than to know your core strengths and who you are. Use them like a bodybuilder, making the "whole you" stronger and more resilient. Work through the resistance and create something better.

I was exposed to ideas I hadn't considered before. I was suddenly able to see, hear and experience life in a way I had not felt since before that first day of boarding school. I was that free child again, nurtured and cared for— but this time, not by my family and village, but by the whole Universe!

I Am Worthy

I began to understand and feel the fundamental truth: all human beings originate from the same Source as everything else. This made it easier for me to detach myself from the need for material goods I had previously craved, owned, and worked to attain.

My new mantra became, "I am worthy. I am here to live a physical experience. The physical body is connected to One Source of Intelligence. The five senses communicate to the physical world and the mental faculties tap into the Power of Awareness."

I began to notice and enjoy the quirky, funny things in life. I became truly absorbed during my walks in nature. I laughed out loud when I finally remembered the time I was living in the village, watching the birds flying in the sky, and how much I would have loved to be as free as them.

Who would have guessed that wild birds would be such a big part of my awakening? However, this time, instead of eating only chicken wings, hoping I would be able to fly, I was asking questions. Who could teach to me to fly high enough to be truly free? What support would I need for that to happen?

I asked the Universe thousands of questions. The deeper I went into the study of myself and the laws of the universe, the closer I was getting to that essence, that unique blueprint that makes up "me." I came to realise that "me" comes from the same energy, is guided by the same consciousness, and is supplied by the same source as the whole Universe. I am not a drop of water— I am the ocean!

Happy To Be Alive

My understanding of other people became more harmonious. Instead of trying to please them, I simply came to understand them better. My physical life was becoming easier. My thoughts were clearer. I could make decisions and work towards goals in a holistic, inclusive way.

It became easier to comprehend the meaning of my studies. I felt better, like a weight was moving away from me. I was happy to be alive. I had no idea where it would take me, but my awareness, and being in the "now" was growing, along with my expanding life experiences.

It hasn't been all plain sailing. Sometimes it was all I could do to resist letting the old beliefs take me back to my old state of fear and lack. But every positive experience overwrote the old programming, meaning that the next one was easier. I was gaining confidence because I was trusting the process of the Universe, steadily moving away from old thought patterns and struggles.

Deliver The Gift You Came To Give

Another surprise: I naturally developed more compassion for people. An understanding of what those around me are going through is now as natural to me as breathing. A core belief I now have is that I believe I was born to keep expanding my knowledge of myself, and in that way, be a teacher to show other people how to do the same for themselves.

I have found the meaning and purpose of my life, distilled into these few words: "Find yourself and deliver to the world the gift you came here to give." I have committed myself to this and I help others to understand how to achieve the same goal.

I have learned to live inside out by understanding my mind. I have learned to meditate, to still my body, and quiet my mind. Just to listen to my inner voice without judgement or comment. It is through the practice of meditation that my old beliefs, placed in my very young mind by frightened people who knew no better, were replaced by true beliefs, full of joy and courage, fully supported by the laws of the Universe.

Confidence

My confidence comes from the same intelligence that makes a bird sing. We trust! We are the same as the bird or the plant. We are the Universe. If I need to get unstuck and bring myself back to the Source of who I am, these thoughts will take me back to the truth. Lack does not exist. We all come from one Source of intelligence, one consciousness, one energy. Can you imagine yourself being able to contemplate being part of this truth?

Thought or Energy comes from this invisible consciousness and governs all universes. The consciousness that has given me life makes a bird fly. It comes from the same source.

There is nothing wrong with us human beings. There is only a lack of awareness.

My big dream was to find who I am. Who is the power behind us?

During the last decade, I have focused on empowering my self-image and changing the perceptions that have been negatively affecting my self-confidence. I have connected with the Infinite and expanded my awareness to restore trust in myself and experience the life I love. I have learned how to face the fears that were holding me back, and explored my inner side to help make confident decisions that are in harmony with my highest good!

Clarity

After receiving deep understanding and positive results for myself, I have been able to coach others to get better clarity and better results for themselves. I no longer need to ask questions like, "Can I really do this?" "What if I'm not good enough?" "What if I lose?" "What if I win?" "Is this really possible?"

Sometimes I don't know where my life will take me, and it is exhilarating and a little scary. But the feeling I get is so good that the ride is well worth the risk.

Being in nature has played a huge part in my awakening. It has reconnected me to Source. I still take long walks in nature, continuously asking questions.

Where I was missing awareness, I now have clarity. Pieces of the puzzle slip more easily into place. My authentic life has started and life is magical. Enter your life, not in conflict with the Universe, but guided to direct your energies into becoming the creative, unique being that you once were.

I have achieved more in the past ten years than the rest of my lifetime. I have become a confident single mother, independent, firmly in charge of my own destiny.

Allow me to show you how to do the same, in a far shorter time frame.

About Martine Lambert

Change is inevitable. Personal growth is a choice. You must put your goals and dreams first. Transform your dreams into reality, goals into achievements, and thinking into results.

Scan the QR code below to request your free audio and 8 thought-provoking questions brochure that warrant your attention. That will start you on the path to the Future You Want.

info@MartineLambert.com

Chapter 3: Activated Living! The Secret to Your Best Quality of Life as You Age | Julie Korte

Have you experienced the loss of a loved family member or friend that has fallen ill? Perhaps you witnessed their body slowly breaking down. Maybe they are sadly no longer with you.

Over 11 years ago, my brother, age 58, left us too soon, when he was diagnosed with Melanoma Cancer. I also watched both my parents suffer through illnesses, leaving us in a way they would not have imagined.

This was the motivation I needed to make a decision. I didn't want my family to see me suffer with illness. This is why I am so passionate about helping people to take control of their own health, to stay away from the sickness industry, and have the best quality of life as they age.

My husband was on medication for several years with a heart issue. His cardiologist said, "Once you start any heart medications, you will be on them for the rest of your life."

For him to gradually reduce and come off this medication is a testimony in itself. What I have implemented into my life over the last several years has had a huge impact and benefited my family.

I have implemented strategies into my family's lifestyle that have enabled me to become more proactive with my own health. This is also easy for you to do!

Expecting To Feel Tired

Many people are happy to go along with life until a tragic health event— heart attack or cancer diagnosis, perhaps.

What if this happened to you someday? Would you be saying to yourself "I need to maintain my health differently."

You might know someone facing a chronic health issue. What if you could help them?

Here's a statement I hear quite often, "It's normal to feel tired and worn out, and we're expected to get these illnesses and diseases, as we age!"

I don't agree with this conclusion. Your body is damaged daily on a cellular level. Imagine if your cells became better capable of coping with the daily stresses and environmental factors, rather than less!

What if you didn't have to ingest a chemical or natural substance? What if your body could combat these stresses and fight on its own?

Would you like better sleep, more energy, less aches and pains? Reduced muscle and joint discomfort, strengthened immunity, less stress, detoxed liver and cells, improved mental focus? Better digestion?

What if you could reduce or avoid the following illnesses and diseases that seem to be taking over many people's lives these days: diabetes, heart disease, cancer, Alzheimer's, dementia, arthritis, MS, asthma, allergies, eczema, psoriasis, auto-immune disorders, chronic fatigue, fibromyalgia, kidney and liver disease, macular degeneration, obesity, high cholesterol, high blood pressure, ADHD, OCD, ASDs (Autism Spectrum Disorders)?

As a society we have all become busier in our lives. All or our schedules are jam-packed. We are eating out more, eating more fast food, consuming more packaged foods, rather than preparing freshly made meals. This might make your life slightly easier, but at what cost to your health?

What changed over these past years? Fifty years ago, when I was a young child, most "modern-day food" we are consuming nowadays was not found in grocery stores, or it was in smaller quantities.

The number of fast-food outlets has grown enormously, along with selections of processed and packaged foods. They contain harmful additives and preservatives. Plus, clever food labelling by manufacturers makes them seem like healthy options.

Unfortunately, they come with added sugar, salt, preservatives, nasty additives and unhealthy seed oils.

200 years ago, the average American consumed only 2 pounds of sugar per year. In 1970, 123 pounds. In 2022, 152 pounds per year. That is 6 cups of sugar per week. You probably don't physically add sugar to your food, but these are hidden in processed foods and shelf staples at supermarkets.

The environment has changed. Electromagnetic Frequencies (EMF's), 3G, 4G, 5G, Bluetooth, Wi-fi, and dirty electricity wreak havoc on your cells.

The air you breathe, water you drink, personal care products you use on your body daily have pesticides, artificial ingredients, GMO's, heavy metals, chemicals, allergens and hormone disruptors. Scientists believe we are exposed to more than 80,000 toxins in our environment.

No wonder so many people are run down, sick, and tired!

Oxidative Stress

Many babies are born with dangerous levels of toxins passed from the mother while still in the uterus. A 2004 study by the Environmental Working Group found that an average of 200 chemicals were in the umbilical-cord blood of some babies. Many of these chemicals are toxic to your brain and nervous system, and can begin the process of infant and childhood cancers. We wonder why children have learning disabilities, hyperactivity, ADHD, OCD, Autism, which once again was hardly heard of back years ago!

Each day, you consume or absorb these toxic products into your body. This creates free radical damage to your cells, creating more inflammation in your body, leading to oxidative stress, known as OS.

Oxidative stress is the breakdown and rusting of your cells, causing cellular damage within your body. Trillions of free radicals bombard your body every day. They attach to the cells, causing them to break down. There's no way to completely avoid OS— it is just part of the natural ageing process. However, when your body's OS stress levels are high, you lack energy, you don't sleep well, you have mild aches and pains, headaches, that "midday slump.".. dragging your feet out of bed.

High oxidative stress is linked to over 200 illnesses and diseases. It impacts every cell, system, tissue, organ, and organism in your body. **Reducing oxidative stress is absolutely critical!**

Here's a metaphor to consider how OS affects your body: imagine an apple. It looks good on the outside, but if you take a bite and leave it, over time, the cells of the apple react with oxygen in the air, resulting in a browning effect. After a while, it looks ugly and rotten!

Inflammation

There is good and bad inflammation. For example, you sprain your ankle. Your ankle becomes hot and red. This is your immune system sending out special inflammatory cells (cytokines) in huge numbers to heal or fight the issue. Then it dies back down.

The bad inflammation is when your immune system sends cells out, but you're not sick, or don't have an issue. This process doesn't stop. It continues to send these cells. You have chronic inflammation and it compounds in your body. You may not feel it— it could be happening silently or manifest physically— for example, annoying aches and pains, arthritis, or it might transition into other illnesses.

The Centers of Disease Control and Prevention state, "Nine of the ten diseases on the top-10 list of causes of mortality, are inflammation-related. Inflammation is on the rise, thanks in part to our more inactive lifestyles, highly processed foods, and a multitude of other factors."

How do you reduce inflammation and OS to protect yourself from getting sick, and feel more energised?

Over the past few years, I have improved my health, and my advice has assisted my family and friends.

Biohacking

Consider small incremental diet and lifestyle changes that create small improvements in your health and life.

My biohacking journey began after a health retreat several years ago. One of our lecturers said, "Your body is an amazing vehicle. Eat and look after it the correct way, and it will look after you." If you add dirty fuel to your car, it will not run efficiently. It may permanently ruin your car. Consider that metaphor when applied to your body.

I swapped out toxic substances for fresh, pesticide-free, organic foods. I mostly shop for groceries at farmer's markets and health shops. Supermarket visits have been somewhat reduced. We also grow some of our own produce. You may not have the space to do this, but it could be your first step to improving your health.

Source healthier options of underarm deodorants, perfumes, toothpaste, mouth washes, hair and body care, toilet sprays and insect sprays. Substitute essential oils for first aid items. Change out dishwashing, dishwasher and laundry detergents for environmentally friendly types. Don't use chemicals when cleaning your home.

Your skin absorbs a huge amount of what you apply to it. Skin care, makeup, lip balms, perfume, hair dyes, sunscreen, nail polishes that I use have either none or very little "nasties" in them. The "Think Dirty" app tells you how toxic your household and personal products are, with a 0 to 10 rating— the lower the number, the less toxic it is.

Your tap water might have chlorine, fluoride and ammonia. Fluoride in water is toxic to your health. Rain water washes off your roof tops, where contaminants collect. Your drinking water should be filtered to ensure you don't add more toxins to your body. Even bottled water can have additives.

Better Food Choices

The next time you eat fast food, processed food, or packaged food, take note. How did it make you feel? Energised? Or, tired, lethargic, wanting a nap? It is easy to grab convenient food without a second thought. Unhealthier foods or products are usually the cheapest.

Unfortunately, when you ingest processed or GMO food, your body doesn't know how to deal with it. It is foreign and unnatural— your system can't absorb it. Another reason why you have less energy, get sick, or gain weight.

Food is not the same as it was years ago— it's not as nutritious as it was back then. Today's modern intensive agricultural methods are stripping nutrients from the soil, leaving produce low in nutritional value. Farmers use more fertilisers on soil and pesticides to spray crops, along with growth hormones and GMO feed is given to livestock and poultry. These factors impact your health. Sourcing or growing your own produce, organically grown without pesticides, is more beneficial for your health, but this is not always easy. Buying organically can be expensive.

We've been told to eat more nutritional foods, eat foods higher in antioxidants, have more sleep, minimise stress or exercise more. Is this the answer? Well partly true but really this has been taken out of our control.

How do you get nutritious foods when produce isn't what it used to be?

Activation

Many people visit the doctor, searching for some miracle pill to take their ailments away. Unfortunately, most doctors don't ask: what's your diet like, what food do you eat, are you physically active? They are happy to prescribe medication, or maybe send you for blood tests, then prescribe medication and some vitamins. This really only addresses the symptoms, rather than the root cause.

Old school methods of supplementing are outdated. This new approach activates your body through a natural pathway called Nrf2. Which takes on a new method of addressing today's health issues. It stimulates your body's ability to fight Oxidative Stress on its own. Nrf2 technology has been studied by the world's most respected scientists and universities.

Washington State University even stated that "**Nrf2 Activation... Potentially the most extraordinary therapeutic and preventative breakthrough in the history of medicine...**"

To take a natural product without toxins, chemicals, or GMO's means you don't have to settle for pills and potions that use decades old technology.

When you are activated, you leverage key nutrients for cellular health, wellness, and longevity.

The only way to reduce free radicals is with antioxidants. Free radicals in your system are not the issue— the issue is having too many.

You cannot replace a nutritious diet with direct antioxidants, but you need good foods to fuel your body. Direct antioxidants work on a 1-to-1 ratio— for each antioxidant molecule, you eliminate one free radical. For example, a punnet of blueberries eliminates about 6,000 free radicals. That sounds good, but remember that your body is bombarded with **trillions** of free radicals every day, so it's not quite enough to keep that balance in check. By activating your body naturally through the Nrf2 pathway, it can produce its own antioxidants at a ratio of 1 million-to-1, instead of 1-to-1. This is a huge deal in helping to keep your health in check.

Consider this: if a fire broke out in your house, would you want to extinguish it with a small cup of water, or would you prefer a fire hose?

My journey to this new world of activation has given me the edge to stay away from the sickness industry and have the ideal best quality of life.

You can have all the money in the world, but without your health, you have nothing.

Success Stories

A friend who has been on the same health journey as me slipped and broke her ankle severely. Her medical team said it would take 18 to 24 months to regain full use of her foot. Instead, after 9 months, she was fully walking again. Her physio was amazed how quick and well she healed. One of the ambulance attendees that picked her up after the accident checked her vitals and remarked that, for a 63-year-old woman, she was one of the healthiest they had seen in some time. He said, "Whatever you are doing, keep doing it!"

A lady I worked with had hypothyroidism, Hashimoto's and pernicious anaemia— she fell asleep at traffic lights— for over 13 years.

She had a racing heart, anxiety, depression, IBS, shakes from the inside out, nausea, heart palpitations, migraines, hair loss, itching. She scratched her feet with an old hair brush until they bled. After being activated and within three days, no racing heart or palpitations, after three months, her eyebrows are growing back and minimal hair loss, her energy levels and mood are improved. Hypothyroid symptoms have disappeared.

Her doctor found her blood work within optimal range. She didn't require her B12 shot. She has her life back and is so grateful she found out about the world of activation.

My personal aches and pains have greatly reduced. My energy levels are better compared to ten years ago. I recover better after group gym workouts. Sleep is more restful. I cope with daily life better. Stress is non-existent. I am not on medication— rare for my age. I am grateful for this quality of life.

Do you want to get to the end of your "work life" to find that you need to spend your "retirement life" visiting doctors, specialists, surgeons, and hospitals? Or, would you prefer to enjoy your later stages of life? You have choices. The decision is yours.

About Julie Korte

Living a better quality of life as you age and stay away from the sickness industry could be as simple as adjusting a few factors in your life to the following:

- Become a Biohacker and remove toxins from your life on a daily basis.
- Eat nutritious and fresh food where possible.
- Check ingredients in what you fuel your body with.
- Get to the root of the cause of aches, pains, ailments causing setbacks in your daily life.
- Repair cellular damage and energise your body
- Most importantly: Activate your Life to reduce Oxidative Stress, Inflammation and Free Radicals.

Julie's Offer

Connect with me on my website at Activated Living where I share more on how to effectively Activate your Life to have better quality of life as you age!

JulieAnnKorte.com

Chapter 4: Adjust Your Sails! Grow, Scale & Thrive in Your Business | Jacqueline Day

I want to help you grow, scale, thrive, and make even more profit. Where are you right now? Maybe you are in a state of fear, afraid there's too much competition, or not enough to go around. You are worried about missing out. You have sleepless nights.

Perhaps you suffer from overwhelm and frustration. There is too much to do. Where do you place your time and energy? Are you storing so much knowledge and responsibility in your head?

Keeping everything in your head creates a bigger spiral of overwhelm, frustration, and anxiety. You have lost direction and do not know what to do next. You despair. You played it safe, and you have regrets.

You feel "quitter's syndrome"— things are not working out, you have worked long hours with little time for anything else, tired, exhausted, wondering if it is all worth it. You feel like just giving up.

If your car has no driver, you can't steer it. If your car has the brakes on, you can't move forward. If your car is stationary, you stay still.

The Perfect Road Map

It does not have to be this way. For many years, I have coached and mentored hundreds of businesses.

Where do you want to be in your business? Visualise yourself with the perfect road map. You are behind the wheel of your car, and your car is working perfectly. You are the driver, you know exactly where you want to go, and how you are going to get there. Something inside you says, "I finally know where I am going." It feels so good.

Picture a time when you had crystal clear clarity and a focused direction. Have that picture in front of you, where you are driving in the right direction. You notice opportunities along the highway. This time, they do not pass you by—they are yours to explore. You are the driver. You know where you are going. You feel excited and have a feeling of certainty about exploring this next opportunity. Imagine you have arrived at your destination. You have achieved your desires, aspirations, and dreams. Every single goal you set, you achieved!

Your dreams have become your reality— everything and more than you could have ever imagined. You drove in the outside lane, overtaking. You were no longer in the inside lane meandering along. You explored with the perfect road map.

Envision yourself with unstoppable momentum. You have success. Your mindset has changed. You have changed. That power inside you increases as you cease to be the Business Operator and become the Business Owner. You have become the leader you were truly meant to be. It feels good, as you look forward to working "on" your business every day with a renewed energy and passion.

If your business is in a state of fear, overwhelm, frustration, anxiety, and you feel like giving up and quitting—you need that road map to figure out where you are going, how to achieve your desires, aspirations and dreams with clarity and unstoppable momentum.

You will get there by understanding how business growth happens so you can grow, scale, and thrive. To get new results, you must do something different. Adjust your sails.

Business Growth

When you create that road map for your business growth, you will overcome your fears. You will know how to respond to obstacles, challenges, and opportunities. You will have a renewed passion which will lead to even more profit.

Imagine that you climb the stairs. You take three steps up. Along comes one of those obstacles. You take two steps back as you deal with the obstacle. You have only taken one step forward. You take another three steps up. Along comes that challenge. As you deal with this challenge, you take another two steps back. You have only taken two steps forward. You climb another three steps. You go back another two steps.

You keep going forward and backward. You are not making the progress you deserve. You are not getting the results that you want. You become tired, frustrated, and overwhelmed.

Next, imagine you step onto an escalator. The only way is up. The journey to the top is smooth. As you meet those obstacles and challenges on the way to the top, those difficulties become less profound. You are open to possibilities and opportunities. Everything works well in your business. You feel on top of the world.

You need to stand out and be unique to meet the competition. COVID caused a world pandemic. Businesses had to adapt, be resilient, and find new ways of working. If you want the success you deserve and you are not achieving it, you need to do something different and adjust your sails. Not next year or next week. Commit to those breakthroughs to grow, thrive, and prosper in your business.

Out of Control

Have you felt the fear of being out of control in your business? In March 2020, John was watching television. Lockdown was announced due to covid. The events and entertainment business had to close. Those were John's only clients.

John's thriving business, providing a product and service to outdoor and entertainment events, disappeared into no business at all.

John had been in business for about three years and was on his way to his first million-pound turnover. He had no income now. Event after event was cancelled. Existing business was cancelled, and no future business was booked. He placed his few staff on furlough, wondering if he should permanently fire them. A voice in his head said, "It's all over. Everything you worked for does not exist anymore. How will you survive this? When will this end?"

John saw no future. Everybody was indoors. There was no life. Everything he had worked for was over. The voice in his head would not go away. "You have had your fun, you have had your good times, you did good business, nothing lasts forever, it has come to an end. Accept it has all ended. Quit while you can." John had "quitter's syndrome" looming over him.

The next few weeks, John doubted he could survive. "I may as well give up. What prospects still exist while in this crisis? This is all the life and business I knew. Will I recover?"

You Are Not Starting From Nothing

John was referred to me for Business Coaching. He was in denial and in doubt, wondering what his future would hold.

I carried out a deep dive into John's Business. I said, "You are not starting from nothing. You have great talent and strengths in your business, far better than your competitors. Do not give up now. Your market has lived in the events and entertainment business. We need to look at your Business Model and see what adjustments we can to future proof your business against any economy or crisis."

I continued, "Tell me about this product and service you offer to the events and entertainment business. What adjustments and innovation can be made and what other markets could this appeal to? What can you do that is unique for these new markets, using your original concepts? Let's look at the new markets first, then at the need they may have, then how you can redesign and innovate this product and service to offer to these new markets. How can you do something different and adjust your sails?"

We worked on new innovation ideas using John's technical expertise so he could get ahead of the curve. Every time we thought of a new market and their need, I asked John, "If there was another world pandemic, would they still need your product and service? Would they need to do business with you?" We would consider entering into that new market if the answer was "yes."

John said, "I will need finance for the software and consultant. I already have cash flow problems."

"John, I know of grants that are available. I can help you with an application. You have an ideal case. We can make a loan application for working capital also.

We mapped out and forecasted John's future. There were more markets and greater insights to go for. We decided he could have a future-proofed business no matter the economy, even if there was a pandemic. He was excited about his future.

The next few months were not always easy. John's associates said, "Surely, you are not carrying on in business when you suffered so much. Find a job! Look what happened to your business!"

John could have let "quitter's syndrome" grip him again, but this was different. We had mapped out a plan. The grant and Working Capital applications were successful. Cash flow was improving. The Software Consultant was hired, and the perfect solution was designed for these new markets.

John obtained his first few contracts. New business came in from new markets with the new innovations that had been applied to John's product and service. John received business from some top brand names. This need would remain no matter what the economy does and even in a world pandemic.

It has been over two years since John approached me for Business Coaching. His business has quadrupled, and he has reached a £3 Million turnover. Next year, he is set to double this. John did something different and adjusted his sails. Imagine what you could achieve if you did the same.

The Business Mastery Escalator Masterclass

My biggest "win" in business is when I see my clients have big wins. I see their businesses grow, scale and thrive. John is one of my many clients who I have shared a big win with.

I love helping my clients to implement the learnings from my many years' experience, from which I have created The Business Mastery Escalator:

MANIFESTING. Every business needs to be creating a future – a crystal clear vision – starting with the end in mind. Many businesses are unclear of what they are capable of manifesting. They fail to see the bigger picture. They lose direction, get stuck, and end up on a different road. My clients benefit from taking a deeper dive into their business.

MODELLING. Many businesses have not thought of "income generating" as being a business model. They miss out on market potential. They miss opportunities— they do not stay ahead of market changes or competition. In this model we find solutions for you to really scale and grow.

MARKETING. Every business needs a marketing strategy or plan to get its message out. Many businesses market because they feel they have to without thinking through why they are doing it, what they are doing, and the real purpose

If this is your strategy, you will not hit the right target audience, you become disappointed, spend money unwisely, and become frustrated. You will not get the results you need for your business. With low or no conversions the business will suffer from low sales and low profits.

With my promotional growth plan, we get clarity on the foundations. We discover who your ideal client is and explore what you need to have the right marketing strategy in place for you.

MAXIMISING. There are many ways you can increase your business revenue and profitability Do you delay your business growth? What about the overwhelm and frustration from not operating fully? We will explore ways you can have true maximization in your business through systems, operations, and optimization to maximize your turnover and sales.

MAPPING. If you need to get somewhere, you need a map. If you don't have one, your competition will get there before you. You will be left behind wondering what went wrong. We will create a new business map that will work whatever the changing conditions are.

We will map out every milestone you need to achieve so you can celebrate your successes along the way.

MATURING. Every business needs to be moving. If you stay still, you go backward. When you go backward, you do not keep pace with the changes that happen around you. You miss out and fail to see opportunities. Get ahead, review, and mature.

When you adopt the habit of working "on" your business instead of "in" your business, you stop being the Business Operator and become the Business Owner— the true leader you are meant to be. I want us to work together so that you can be my next "win" when your business grows, scales, and thrives.

About Jacqueline Day

Jacqueline is a Master Coach qualified in Personal Development Coaching, and Business Coaching and a Master Practitioner of Neuro-Linguistic Programming. She is an Award-Winning Coach, Mentor, Award Winning Author, and International Speaker.

She has coached hundreds of businesses and leaders in sectors to grow, scale, and thrive. Her biggest "win" is when her clients have the breakthroughs to achieve the success they deserve to get to the next level.

She will be your soundboard and powerful supporter. Her coaching style is open and non-judgemental, based upon trust and confidentiality. Coaching with Jacqueline will be enjoyable, motivational, and purposeful. Her Coaching will empower you with the focus and accountability to enable you to consistently achieve the results you want and deserve.

Jacqueline's Offer

Discover the 5 Power Steps to Transform Your BELIEF For B.U.S.I.N.E.S.S Success.

Are your belief patterns serving you well in business? When you discover these 5 Power steps, you will make transformations that will have an empowering impact on your business's success. Developing a success mindset will set you up to win in business, and you too will make an impact as you become self-aware and start to make the change for even better results in your business.

StrategicPerformanceCoaching.com/BELIEF

Chapter 5: Work From Home! Build An Online Business To Support Your Lifestyle, Retirement & Legacy | Ian Cory

What hopes and dreams have seemed to stick with you for many years, but they remained just that... *dreams?* For a long time, I *dreamed* of running a successful home-based business, but I always approached it with a cautious eye. Perhaps you can relate? Being curious and cautious about the future, stuck in learning mode, hesitant to take action, and claim your future?

I'll be honest: recent economic developments have shaken me to my core, making me realise it was finally time to build my online business. Perhaps you have been "stuck in between"— not quite happy (or fulfilled), but also not quite motivated to make a change. What are you waiting for? It's time to embrace the fear, blow past the excuses, and pursue your greatness with urgency.

Our Generation's Greatest Fear

If you're like me and grew up without the internet, social media, and smartphones, you know how much the world has changed. The pace of life is dizzying, and it's tough to keep up. But here's the rub: the older we get, the harder it becomes to keep pace with these technological advancements.

Did you know that more and more 50-year-olds are being forced to delay retirement until their early 70s? That's a staggering amount of extra time in the workforce, and it's not always by choice. With automation, artificial intelligence, downsizing, ageism, and unforeseeable events like recessions, our once-secure futures hang in the balance.

It's time to take charge of your life and make your dreams a reality. If you are nearing retirement, you have a lot on your mind. Financial security is one of your top concerns. The "baby boomer" generation's biggest fear is not death or illness, but poverty in old age— outliving our savings, barely surviving from an inadequate pension.

You Must Adapt To This Changing World

Do you have a diminishing sense of financial security and anxiety about a future which no longer promises unconditional progress? Job security is becoming a thing of the past with all of the financial consequences that entails. If your retirement no longer seems far away, your world is an increasingly uncertain place.

To successfully prepare for the future, you must understand your future challenges. You also need to identify what needs to change and what doesn't.

In order to grow, you must adapt and embrace new challenges that will help you develop. Without growth, you stagnate. Whether you like it or not, change will happen. You can resist it and be left behind, or embrace it and grow through these changes.

What prevents you from success? Fear, which is inarticulate, until you give it form by way of excuses not to act.

Change is scary. It means venturing into the unknown, dealing with uncertainty which makes you feel insecure and afraid. This fearful self-suggestion accumulates. You become subject to a sort of self-hypnosis.

Hypnosis is, "A trance-like state that resembles sleep but is induced by a person whose suggestions are readily accepted by the subject." You are hypnotised by ingrained beliefs about yourself, other people, the world, money, business, the past, or the future.

Your greatest enemy is your subconscious self. You live within your comfort zone— your beliefs are limiting (negative) rather than liberating (positive). While your subconscious self imprisons you, preventing you from making positive changes, it acts in your best interest, protecting you from what it perceives as harm.

Fear = False Expectations Appearing Real

Fear is an effective hypnotist and can stop you in your tracks, from doing what would otherwise improve your life. Whether you ask for a pay raise, move home to start a new job, or you start a business, fear is ready to intervene and cut you off at the pass. A constricting inertia then resumes control of your life.

You are more successful than you realise. You have survived until now and are therefore the result of your adaptability to circumstances. Leaving home for the first time, a promotion at work, getting married, raising a family, have all involved adjustments to your reality, which you have taken in stride. These are positive and welcome changes!

Repurpose the adaptability that served you in the past, to creatively provide for a financially secure future. It's time to change your inner hypnotist.

There are people working less than half your hours, making ten times the money. To create your secure and prosperous future, take a different approach to achieve a life free from financial anxieties in retirement.

Imagine being in a position where you can help your children with the financial challenges they face— for example, affording a mortgage at a time when home ownership is largely unobtainable.

Job = Just Over Broke

It took me a while to accept that, apart from winning the lottery or inheriting a windfall from a relative, I would never become wealthy trading my time for money, working for someone else at a J.O.B. (Just Over Broke!) There had to be a better way to create a sustainable income to replace and exceed my day job.

Like many others, I was caught up in the rat race, doing what I didn't enjoy, trading time for money. I knew there were those who had built successful home-based businesses but I never had the confidence or the know-how to do the same.

I knew about experts who had started internet businesses. Emails invited me to two- and three-day seminars, where a succession of established internet marketing gurus evangelised how it was possible for the average person to build an online business from home, transforming their financial circumstances.

Unlike traditional high street "brick-and-mortar businesses"— these required no salaried employees, capital, equipment, inventory, or supply chains.

Welcome To The World Of Internet Marketing

If internet marketing had existed when I was a young adult, my life would have been transformed beyond recognition. Fast-forward several decades. I thought the world of websites was for innovative players such as Amazon while "blogs" were for techies and "geeks." I saw the whole thing as a fad which would pass once the online novelty wore off. How wrong I was!

Habits of thought can prevent people like you and me from making changes and learning new skills.

The Potential And Accessibility Of The Internet For US Individual Home-Based Entrepreneurs

You don't need to be a mechanic to drive a car. Likewise, you do not need to be technically minded to start your internet marketing business. You are already a computer user today— PCs, laptops, iPads, and tablets are as common as wristwatches. Do not get overwhelmed by the "means" of your online marketing business— focus on the "ends" including:

Low start-up costs. Start your business today with low start-up costs compared to traditional brick-and mortar businesses. In the early stage, you don't need employed staff to administer or pay. Scale your business later!

Ability to work from home. Work from any location with internet access, on a beach or up a mountain, using your smartphone.

Flexibility. Set your own schedule. You can have more control over your time. You can balance your work and personal life in a way that is impossible with a traditional 9-5 job.

Multiple streams of income. Your online business allows you to create more than one source of income and increase financial stability.

Follow your passion. Work on something you enjoy.

There are always new growth opportunities on the internet. As you learn, grow your business and generate more income.

To Start, You Don't Even Need Your Own Products!

The opportunities to promote the products of others through affiliate marketing have never been as great as they are today and these are increasing all the time. Generate passive income (commissions) for years— a useful form of retirement income!

Financial freedom is exciting and compelling, and has existed for centuries. For me, it means being able to spend my time as I please, working only if I want to, doing what I find personally rewarding. To live the life

I want without worrying about money. It means being able to travel and take holidays when I choose, without any boss's permission. It means having the freedom to live life on my own terms.

I attended many exciting seminars and bootcamps—many times, buying programs promoted by the speakers. My problem was that I was still sceptical. I knew the methods worked, but I lacked the self-belief that they would work for me. I had never done anything like it before.

The Past Does Not Equal The Future

I read motivational books by Tony Robbins, Darren Hardy, Brian Tracy, Napoleon Hill, Claude Hopkins, Ted Nicholas, David Ogilvy, Drayton Bird, Perry Marshall, Russell Brunson, Paul O'Mahony, Nick James, and Bob Bly. I learned about product funnels, traffic generation, landing pages, email marketing, copywriting, affiliate marketing, and joint venture partnerships.

By immersing myself in these books, seminars, webinars, and podcasts, I realised that what was stopping me from moving forward and starting a business wasn't a lack of knowledge, but my mindset!

My thoughts and attitudes were governed by conventional thinking. I was afraid to go beyond the comfortable and the familiar. When I read about someone who had succeeded with their online business, I would instinctively think of reasons why it wouldn't work for me. I would be creative in my excuses. I have no product to sell, I don't have the capital to get started, and the internet market has already been cornered. I could always think of an obstacle. I feared taking the first steps.

I Persisted In My Education!

I read more books by entrepreneurs and successful salespeople. I attended webinars. I watched TED talks on YouTube. One day, I opened an email from Pat Mesiti about his upcoming online Wealth Evolution program. I first encountered Pat at a three-day marketing seminar in London in 2018. Pat is a compelling speaker. I was impressed with his presentation, focusing exclusively on mindset and attitude.

I signed up for his webinar series and the Best Coaching Academy program of his joint venture partner David Cavanagh. I realised a multitude of easy to use software tools made the process of online marketing, website building, attracting customers, creating and managing product offerings as easy and as fun as playing a computer game.

The obstacles I created began to dissolve. I realised that making money online was possible. Thousands of ordinary people just like me were succeeding, where I had previously feared to tread. I rejected the obstacles and turned my attention to possibilities.

I decided to focus on affiliate marketing, promoting other peoples' products to earn a commission, sometimes over 40 percent per sale. You don't have to create your own product, or the marketing materials. The product owner handles customer service queries. You get paid for upsells, so when a customer pays to upgrade the product, or renew their subscription, you get more commissions, sometimes for years.

Affiliate Marketing Evangelism

You too consume products and services. You may become evangelists and recommend these to others. This is where affiliate marketing is useful and profitable for you. As your knowledge and experience grows, you increase your income further by becoming an online marketing coach.

You can benefit from the convenience of running your online business from a single platform. You can create web pages, emails, manage your autoresponder, track your sales and link to social media from the same place without using multiple tools. You can create drag and drop web pages, even comprehensive libraries of simple tutorial videos.

Do what I have done: gain the knowledge you need. Take that first step to securing a financially secure and comfortable future. You don't need to know everything to get started, as I originally thought. **You can learn as you build.** Join a mentor's program, someone who has succeeded and is where you would like to be. It is your fastest and easiest route to success.

About Ian Cory

Ian spent 12 years in the Royal Navy before steering a complete change of course into civilian life. A further 17 years in the I.T. Industry swapping a lot of time for money included working stints in the Middle East and Europe.

After being "downsized" following the dot.com crash at the turn of the Millennium, Ian worked in a variety of roles swapping yet more time for money in telemarketing, customer service and IT support. He then spent 13 years working in payroll and software training.

Ian has now decided to adopt the swapping money for time model with affiliate and YouTube video marketing.

Ian enjoys reading history, watching football, and any films starring Lee Marvin or Sean Connery.

Ian's Offer

To give you a flavour of the sort of feature rich platform available to make your online marketing life easier, you can sign up for a free account at the website below. There are lots of free video tutorials and other resources including a free e-book. If you decide to go further, there is a menu of upgrade options to suit your needs and plans.

QRCodes.pro/1lxZHE

Chapter 6: Allow Your Dream! The Secret Formula For Body, Mind & Spiritual Success | Billie Wilde

What dreams hide within you? Dreams can come true, but they are not guaranteed. Your mind can carry your dreams into reality, allow your dreams to slip away, or worse— drive them away. You can be your own worst enemy.

You own your own mind, decisions, feelings, and actions. The problem is that other (usually well-meaning) people think they know what is best for you. "They" think it's their job to protect you from yourself. "They" say you are trying to go beyond what is right for your education or status.

The time has come to unapologetically own your mind. It is yours. Get to know it. Become friends with it. You will profit in many ways from this friendship. If you can calm your body, and listen to your mind, then the real you (that you were meant to be) can express itself and live without fear. You can accomplish anything!

Change Your Picture

Do you feel that you are "talked over" or ignored in meetings, boardrooms, discussion groups? Are you a teacher who does not control your space?

Perhaps you have a lot of knowledge, but an associate of yours does all the talking, takes all the accolades, and gets the promotions you deserve?

Do you have a panic attack when asked to speak in front of a group, or onstage with a microphone?

If you need to speak for long periods of time, do you frequently lose your voice?

Do you aspire to be a performer? singer, actor, dancer, advertising voice over, radio announcer, master of ceremonies?

If you do not present to your audience with the confidence and joy that you would like, then you are lacking full "ownership" of your ability. To change your picture, you must take action, do the work, embrace, develop, and own it. Only then you can "allow your dream."

Deep Breathing

When you feel stressed or upset (driving in traffic or dealing with a difficult child) begin with this amazing physical trick with your body. Once you conquer this (with practice) you can change your state of being.

Most people breathe shallowly into the top of their lungs. This is pre-set in early childhood, encouraged by well-meaning kindergarten teachers. Do remember this? Your teacher said, "Come along children, let's take a deep breath. Here we go. Breathe in. Chest out. Tummy in. Breathe out." Wrong! That is not a "deep breath."

The widest part of your lung's structure is the lower section—the upper part is much narrower. My magic word is "allow." At first, it takes consciously thinking about whether you are allowing the air through to the bottom of your lungs. Free your ribcage. Relax.

Take that lovely, relaxing, deep breath in, to the bottom of your lungs. Let your shoulders go. Release tightness. Breathe in through your nose to a slow count of four. Hold for a moment. Breathe out through your mouth to a slow count of five.

Check your shoulders and see if you feel a difference in your state of being. Hopefully you are calmer and gently under control.

There is a lot more to this process, but this is your introduction. Filling your lungs to the bottom.

The Jaw and Posture

When you make a first impression, nothing presents an "air of confidence" like great posture. If your body is in-line, head up, facing forward, ears positioned directly above your relaxed shoulders, straight spinal column, legs straight but relaxed, feet firmly placed on the ground, you will appear to any onlooker like you "mean it"— whatever "it" is.

Find a stretch of ground or floor where you can comfortably take ten steps. Clench your teeth hard together and walk those ten steps. Turn around, unclench your jaw, relax your shoulders, and walk back.

You will notice a dramatic difference in comfort level. When you tighten your jaw, you also tighten the position receptors in the temporal region and inner ear at the back and top of the neck. This in turn tightens the postural muscles. The sensory receptors in the bottom of your feet also react, since a fear of falling affects your posture. A clenched jaw is a visible sign of stress.

My Dad would say, "Free voice and free posture are inseparable." I say, "Just stay loose."

You perform every task much better when you are relaxed, so these jaw exercises are very important. Your effort and persistence will reward you and your audience.

The pivotal points of your jaw are the temporomandibular joints. The temporal bone is at the temple and the mandibular bone is at the jaw. The point at which these two bones meet is the temporomandibular joint.

As with all joints throughout the body, there is a layer of cartilage between these bone joints to allow the freedom of movement required for chewing, swallowing, breathing, yawning, articulation, etc., in cooperation with the associated muscles.

When we are about to use joints and muscles to exercise our bodies, we usually stretch them before we perform any extreme activity. However, not many people consider the temporomandibular joints and associated muscles. Consequently, these joints become stiff and resistant to movement, especially when exacerbated by mental stress and the "clenching" of the jaw.

Whenever I do something stressful, I perform an exercise to stretch (relax) the jaw.

Become Aware When You Are Stressed

You and I live in varying degrees of stress. Take into consideration responsibilities, mortgages to pay, children's problems, parent's problems, cost of living rising, value of dollar dropping. The big question to ask yourself is, "Will my stress make any difference?"

Stressing has caused me to be unable to effectively look at possible solutions. I am convinced that my breast cancer was caused by the terrible stress I experienced in the months before the cancer was discovered. Thank heavens for an early diagnosis!

Awareness is the beginning of change. Without "true recognition" there is no change.

Take a lovely, deep breath and try to relax.

A tight jaw is the instant, natural hindbrain (cerebrum) reaction to any form of stress or shock— door slamming, any sudden noise, driving in dangerous traffic, a tyrannosaurus rushing across the park at you.

Try wriggling your jaw gently from side to side a few times, then gently dropping it down and lift back up a few times. Repeat. "Gently" is the operative word.

Don't be surprised if you realise that your jaw is resisting this process— it's likely to resist because this is probably unknown territory. This resistance is what we are talking about: a tight jaw. Take that lovely deep breath again.

You might like to consider, when breathing in through your nose, to gather all negative thoughts and feelings from your brain and exhale them gently through your mouth. Smile and say, "Goodbye negativity." The day can change from that moment on.

Stand in front of a mirror, preferably full length, relaxed shoulders, jaw gently "flopped open" as if you were asleep. Cup your lower jaw with your dominant hand, thumb toward one ear and forefinger toward the other. Gently apply pressure taking your lower jaw straight backwards, not down, stopping the moment resistance is felt. Hold that position with the small resistance for 30 seconds. Release and repeat four times.

If you are in a situation where you need to stretch your jaw and there are other people around you, just do it. Your need is more important than their gaping wonderment at your actions. Smile sweetly at them and say, "I see that you are wondering what I am doing. I am stretching my temporomandibular joints. Doesn't everybody?"

You might have seen high level athletes perform "pre-event" rituals. This exercise is one of them, especially for running. These people know the importance of "staying loose" and that this "not so quick tip" helps to keep them there, well balanced.

The Five W's

Now that you have taken steps to get your body to cooperate, get your mind working for you instead of against you. My beautiful friend and mentor, Pat Mesiti, asks confronting questions to make me stay on track and analyse my actions. In other words, make it real.

My answer to self-analysis is a play on the "Five W's"—Who, What, When, Where, Why, followed by the clincher, which is How.

When you feel doubt or hesitation, ask yourself, what are you doing to help people? What problem are you solving? Why are you helping that person? The answer for me: I love to solve is people's fear of all things "stage!" No matter what the forum.

I had to live through terror for the first six months of my career in "showbiz!" I can now prevent anyone else from having this terrible feeling of fear and anxiety.

I was accepting that fear as "par for the course", until one day, at a "Bert Newton Show," I was prowling around backstage in my usual state of terror waiting for my call to camera. Barry Crocker, a doyen and statesman of the industry, walked up to me. He said, "What are you doing? Every time we are on the same show, I witness your bizarre ritual. Are you frightened? Why?"

I said, "Yes. I am always worried that something might go wrong in front of millions of people! Aren't you even a little bit concerned?"

Barry said, "No, I am not. You shouldn't be, either. I watched your excellent rehearsal. Get out there and enjoy the fact that you are making lots of people happy. You know your stuff, now give it to them. Step aside from yourself and give it to them."

That changed my life. I accepted my knowledge of the situation and purred like a kitten every time I was on whatever kind of stage.

If you own your "stuff" then you have every right to deliver it with joy and confidence, wherever and to whomever you choose.

Staying Loose

Self-empowerment allows you to own yourself: your decisions, actions, ethics, desires and dreams. This is available if you are willing to take the necessary steps to confront your past influences and influencers full on, allowing you to work toward your personal goals with integrity and full ownership of your brain.

It takes guts for you to realise those moments when you need to confront someone. To get to your goal, the first person you need to honestly confront, is you.

Often, we believe that it's better (easier) to "go with the flow" of others think we should do or be, than to go against the grain toward what our hearts are aching for. Our personal dreams and desires are gathered up and placed somewhere in the recesses of our minds, to be ignored. This road is neither better, nor easier.

It is never too late to change, and own, your mind.

Mother And Daughter

A very clever, witty, beautiful, British girlfriend of ours had her mother visiting from England. She wanted to bring her to Sydney and asked if they could stay with us for a few days. We were delighted, looking forward to meeting her mother, who had never been to Sydney before. Our home sat on the Parramatta River, looking across the water straight into Bicentennial Park— a stunning environment for a visitor.

The Mother told me that she loved to sing when she was a child, but when she was 7 years old and tried out for the school choir, the music teacher said she was off key, had no sense of pitch, she should never try to join a choir again, and was asked to leave the room. She was devastated and never sang again, until that day, at age 70.

I was amazed. I was hearing a lyrical voice that showed no signs of tone deafness. I dragged her into my studio and said, "I don't believe this. We will work this out." After a few terrified objections, we worked on The Application of Pitch!

20 minutes later, she was singing every note that I played, with perfect pitch. We sang one of her favourite songs, which she performed to perfection.

She was stunned and I was delighted. Her Daughter tells me that, to this day, she hasn't stopped singing. The Mother says she is making up for the 63 years she missed out on singing.

School music teachers, who know music, need to learn how to teach children to apply pitch. Only one in a million people are actually tone deaf. Let us help the world to sing out loud.

Meet Jodie

Jodie was born into an interesting family. Her parents were professional classical singers—father a baritone and mother a coloratura soprano. They sang at The Tivoli Theatre in Melbourne, performing wonderful duets. Being extremely good looking helped a lot.

Jodie's mother had been singing professionally on radio since she was 5 years old, but decided she didn't want to sing any more. She wanted to focus on family.

Her father was devastated and began to drink heavily. He was brought up Mormon and was a Mormon Lay-preacher. This behaviour was against all the rules. He was an angry alcoholic.

Jodie's first memory of the world was being reefed out of bed in the middle of the night, plonked unceremoniously on the kitchen bench, with her brother on one side and her sister on the other and forced to watch while her father beat her mother, declaring, loudly, that this was what happened to sluts! Jodie said her mother was an angel.

Life in this household was Hell! The family would wait for father's car to come into the driveway, listen to the way the car door closed, then the steps to the front door, the way the door was closed, and the steps in the hallway. The tension could change in a nano-second.

Jodie and her mother were prime targets— the others were rarely touched. At age 7, Jodie was thrown down the stairs, landing in hospital. It was amazing she didn't die.

Jodie was a born singer, but she didn't dare to sing because there would always be something wrong with it, and punishment would follow.

When he was sober, Jodie's Dad was wonderful. This was her real dad and she loved him dearly. At age 8, Jodie realised her father's anger had nothing to do with her, or her mother. It was anger at and within himself.

Fast forward to age 11. Jodie was studying Freud and Jung, determined to understand the Human Condition. At 13, she studied law, to tell her mother what she could legally do to stop the behaviour. Mother finally charged him, took him to court, but dropped the charges. Jodie was devastated.

On Jodie's 16th birthday, her father insisted on a birthday party. She was horrified! She never invited anyone home because she didn't know what might happen. Nobody knew about the home situation. It was a secret!

He put on the best party and all of Jodie's friends thought the sun shined out of him.

Three days later, he came through the door and launched himself in Jodie's direction. The family was at the dining table having dinner. Jodie, staying loose, knew what she had to do. She had rehearsed it. She stood up, looked him full in the face and said, "Dad, make the bruises on my legs, or arms, or face, please. He exploded, "What are you on about?" She kept his gaze and remained as calm as she possibly could, believing that she might be dead at any minute.

"I don't want to have to take off my clothing for the photographs," she stated softly. He began to lumber toward her shouting expletives. Jodie maintained her space and said, with more volume and total conviction, "Know it, Dad! I am going to charge you."

He abruptly stopped, did a double take, tried to frighten her with an evil glare, to which she said, "Know it, Dad. I am 16 years old. I know my rights. I will charge you!"

He took one step toward her. She raised herself to her full 173 centimeters, maintaining eye contact. He stopped, waited a moment, turned on his heel, lumbered back out through the door, got back into the car, and drove away.

Jodie turned to her family and said, "There! You just saw it. I have been trying to tell you. He is a bully, and bullies are cowards."

He never hit her again. They became best friends to the end of his life. Jodie won the Grand Finals of two major television singing competitions, has enjoyed a long career on television and stage, in Australia and Internationally, and still graces many a stage. She concluded she could own her fear, deal with it, put her demons to rest and allow her dream. You can too!

By the way, this wasn't about Jodie. It was me!

About Billie Wilde

I love to watch light bulbs and epiphanies exploding around my clients as we work together on their individual problems with anything (or everything) to do with "stage!"

Together, we turn it around to joyful knowledge and ownership of the process, resulting in confident and successful presentations/performances.

BillieWilde.com

Chapter 7: Knowledge! Your Spirituality, Happiness, Freedom And Success Is All About What You Know | Dr. Gerald Nyasulu

I was born in Malawi, in the poorest district in the poorest country in the entire world. Growing up, all I felt was a lack of confidence, low self-esteem, and a lack of direction. Growing up in this environment limited my life. Life and achievement expectancy was grim. With the odds stacked against me, I worked hard in school, learning as much as I could. Life was still confusing. I had lots of disturbing and annoying questions that would never go away.

You can relate to how my life was when I was growing up. Culture has taught us to put up a cheerful face, but inwardly, we are eaten by a burning desire to amount to something. We are besieged by circumstances that we feel powerless to change. The odds are stacked against us to the extent that we have surrendered to fate and gotten on with the flow. Your life does not have to continue being average. You have a once-in-a-lifetime opportunity to turn things around for good in your life.

The Questions That Were Eating Me

On the surface, I looked happy, like any other teenager in my boys-only boarding high school. However, inwardly, questions were eating me up. **Who am I? Where did I come from? Why am I here? When I die, what will I find out there? Of all these religions, which one is the true religion?**

I seemed unable to shake off these questions. I was desperate. I had to quickly find answers. I had to understand and resolve these questions!

I was not the only one asking these questions. Many people in my age group had equal confusion. They were searching, but for what? No one seemed to know or understand. We were all on the search.

Life gets confusing and repetitive. You can either bury these questions by keeping yourself busy with life, drown these annoying and nagging questions. Or you can man up and face these questions head-on! I chose the latter. I chose to confront these questions head-on! I chose courage over fear. I chose to find the courage and explore the questions that would resolve all my confusion and doubts.

I Had To Find The Truth

It required three years of serious reading and research. I had enough of keeping my head in the sand and walking in pretence. I had to find and know the truth. I gave myself permission to study the main religions and their beliefs. I read their sacred books and asked difficult questions to the scholars and practitioners of those religions.

The more I searched, the more I felt empty and desperate. That emptiness was a painful and excruciating pain, like a physical wound.

I realised one fundamental truth: **knowledge is the key to everything in life.** Where there is no knowledge, people make silly, sometimes fatal, mistakes.

Twenty-Eight Years Later

At the end of the search, I had a major encounter that changed my life forever. On July 26, 1994, I encountered God, the one who loved me and died for me. I came face to face with the raw power of God. My life took a turn that no one would deny the supernatural evidence of the manifestation of grace. The divine enablement would catapult me beyond the conceivable.

Every day for three months after the initial encounter, as it was in the Garden of Eden, God would come in the cool of the day and teach me the Truth as relayed in the Bible. I learned and experienced the knowledge. I would later find what He taught me in the Scriptures many years later as I began studying the

Bible. I am still unpacking what He taught me in three months!

Where that knowledge has taken me is phenomenal. It is a miracle. From humble beginnings to managing a multimillion-dollar ministry full of signs and wonders! Miracles are real, and still take place today. My ministry started with only three members in 2007 in the small town of Townsville in North Queensland. What was the secret? Knowledge.

The Centrality Of Knowledge In Your Life Cannot Be Oversized

Knowledge produces belief and frames your perception. Perception is your ability to see or hear the world around you and your thoughts. When your knowledge is limited, it leads to limited sight and hearing. One can easily misconstrue a simple thing simply because of a problem with their perception. If this is true, then it also follows that the reverse is also true. When someone's knowledge is not accurate or wrong, it leads to misconception. People have misconstrued statements or actions simply because they have the wrong information. Jesus said:

Mat 6:22. The light of the body is the eye: if therefore thine eye be single, thy whole body shall be full of light.

Mat 6:23. But if thine eye be evil, thy whole body shall be full of darkness. If therefore the light that is in thee be darkness, how great is that darkness!

Knowledge is forceful, and it causes people to act in certain ways. Ignorance is equally forceful. Human beings act based on the knowledge that we have accumulated from the time of our birth. There are times we fail to take advantage of unfamiliar opportunities because they are outside of our knowing. Ignorance can force us to act in certain ways because we lack understanding of the new situation.

Knowledge Controls Your Perception

Perception is the position one holds derived from the totality of information available through the five natural senses. I like giving an example of food. When I travel, I like to taste the local food. Within my work of ministry, when I do home visitations, I love tasting my host's local foods. I have tasted all sorts of foods that I ordinarily wouldn't have tasted.

As I embarked on the freedom I enjoy now, I had to make up my mind giving myself permission to whatsoever shall be set before me, and I shall eat and enjoy it the way the locals enjoy it. That conclusion came from a simple instruction that our Lord Jesus Christ gave the Apostles when He was sending them to preach the gospel.

In Luke chapter 10, verses 7 and 8, it is recorded:

Luke 10:7. And in the same house remain, eating and drinking such things as they give: for the labourer is worthy of his hire. Go not from house to house.

Luke 10:8. And into whatsoever city ye enter, and they receive you, eat such things as are set before you:

Jesus instructed His disciples to eat whatever was set before them. It is easy to assume that since they were all Jewish, they would have the same type of food. That's a good assumption, but Jesus is aware that food is what your mother taught you.

These disciples came from different backgrounds. There were foods for poor people, and there were foods for the rich. Those who grew up in wealthy households had foods that would have been unfamiliar to those from poor households. In the same vein, those who grew up in poor households would have been taught to eat certain foods which were unfamiliar to the folk from wealthy households.

Food is what your mother introduced you to. When you eat foods from childhood, it becomes a part of your knowledge, and you do not have any problem with it at all. However, if someone from a different background was presented with what you consider a delicacy, you will be shocked to notice that they may even throw up. The act of throwing up has nothing to do with the food in front of them. It has everything to do with a lack of knowledge.

Many times, people have eaten new foods and thanked the chef for such a delicious meal. However, the moment they have been made aware that they just ate something that they consider inedible, dirty, or unholy, their gag reflex kicks in. They feel nauseated and can throw up.

Travel Experiences

I never knew there were other seafoods besides fish until I arrived in Australia in 2004. I landed in the lovely seacoast of Townsville, and you can imagine my shock at being confronted with many seafoods.

I reflected on my own "delicacies" back home in Malawi. I love flying insects, beetles, locusts, and mice. For me, these are delicacies. I looked at prawns, seashells, bugs, and crabs, and concluded that if Australian mothers taught children that this was food, that was why they ate it. I hesitated. My mother never taught me that this was food, because it didn't exist in Malawi. Since I had decided to eat whatever was set before me, I enjoyed eating seafoods, even though I was the only one in my household eating the seafood.

This shows the power of knowledge and the power of ignorance. Imagine if we were to scale it up to the spirit realm. There are many things in your spiritual walk you had labelled demonic and satanic when in it was the demonstration of the power of God. You might have even lauded demonstrations of the supernatural when they were demonic!

Where is the boundary? Knowledge is the boundary. If one has the right knowledge of God and how He operates by His Spirit, you will be quick to try and discern that one demonstration is of God and the other not. In this context, one does not need the gift of discerning spirits, but rather, **discernment by knowledge.**

1 John 4:1. Beloved, believe not every spirit, but try the spirits whether they are of God: because many false prophets are gone out into the world.

1 John 4:2. Hereby know ye the Spirit of God: Every spirit that confesseth that Jesus Christ is come in the flesh is of God.

1 John 4:3. And every spirit that confesseth not that Jesus Christ is come in the flesh is not of God, and this is that spirit of antichrist, whereof ye have heard that it should come, and even now already is it in the world.

What's the standard for discernment? Knowledge. Once you know the test, it's easy to arrive at the right conclusion. If a spirit confesseth that Jesus Christ comes in the flesh, then it is of God, and any spirit that denies that Jesus Christ is come in the flesh is not of God, and the Bible calls that the spirit of the antichrist!

How simple is that? How did one discern? By knowledge and not the gift of discernment. You cannot afford to live life any longer without having solid knowledge of the Word of God. Get guesswork out of your life and walk with God. Don't be presumptuous.

Act With Confidence From A Place Of Solid Knowledge

This is how God put it: "My people are destroyed for lack of knowledge: because thou hast rejected knowledge, I will also reject thee, that thou shalt be no priest to me: seeing thou hast forgotten the law of thy God, I will also forget thy children." — Hosea 4:6 (KJV)

Knowledge controls your perception, and your perception controls your emotions and feelings. How often have you heard children of God talk about how they feel? I am not trying to discredit feelings, but I am showing you how unreliable your feelings are. They are like shifting castle houses on the seashore!

Feelings shift like clouds in the sky which are driven by the wind. Feelings are like the temperature of the day, which shifts during the course of the day, due to various factors. Feelings are like smoke which now is and later disappears when the wind blows upon it. Feelings are shifty like the waves of the sea.

You cannot build your life on feelings. This is the primary cause of circus marriages today. They all have one thing in common: feelings!

I feel that we have connected. I feel that there is chemistry. I don't have feelings for you anymore. When the feeling has shifted like the sand on the seashore, what happens? Separation and divorce follow. Therefore, feelings are unreliable to be the basis for any decision in life. Knowledge is more reliable and stable. When you know that you know, and decide based on that knowing, your decision lasts the test of time.

As A Child Of God, You Are Called To Act Based On Knowledge

Knowledge is the sure foundation of faith. Faith which springs in your spirit based on solid knowledge. Any attempt to believe based on one's feelings is what our Lord Jesus Christ told us that it is self-deception.

Matthew 7:24. Therefore whosoever heareth these sayings of mine, and doeth them, I will liken him unto a wise man, which built his house upon a rock.

Matthew 7:25. And the rain descended, and the floods came, and the winds blew, and beat upon that house; and it fell not: for it was founded upon a rock.

Matthew 7:26. And every one that heareth these sayings of mine, and doeth them not, shall be likened unto a foolish man, which built his house upon the sand.

Matthew 7:27. And the rain descended, and the floods came, and the winds blew, and beat upon that house; and it fell: and great was the fall of it.

Notice the difference between these two individuals. They both hear the sayings of our Lord Jesus Christ. However, one "doeth them" and one "doeth them not." Don't get caught up in the jargon of the scriptures and high-sounding theological hermeneutics of this simple passage. Every detail is the same except that one "doeth them" while the other "doeth them not." They face identical challenges.

The only question to ask ourselves is what does it mean when Jesus says one "doeth them" while the other "doeth them not?" The Greek word used there for "doeth" is poieō. This Greek word occurs 576 times in the KJV Bible and has been translated by forty-five different English words!

It's crazy trying to sort out the exact meaning that Christ wanted to convey to his listeners. I will not bother you with the different shades of meanings this word carries. The meaning that Christ wanted to convey in this context was exercising or practising if you wish.

It Is Not Natural

Imagine a student who attends math class, and the teacher demonstrates how to solve an algebra problem. He understands but refuses to practise solving the algebra problems the teacher has provided to the class. He assures himself that he has understood and will be okay during exams in six months.

His fellow students complete the homework provided by the teacher. When they make mistakes, the teacher corrects them and re-explains them until they have perfected their grasp of the algebra concepts. What are the chances that our students who refused to do the exercises and practice the maths problems would get everything right during exams? It will take more than a miracle to pass!

Our Lord and Saviour Jesus Christ understands that it is not natural for you to love others unconditionally. He understands it is not natural for you to turn the other cheek when someone hits you on one. He understands it is not natural to change your perceptions overnight.

He gives you a way out: exercise and practice.

Imagine an athlete preparing for a marathon, who hires a personal trainer. They meet up to train several months before a competition. Each time they meet, the trainer demonstrates certain marathon running techniques, and the athlete assures the personal trainer that he has understood, and never practices.

Several months pass, and the competition date arrives! He puts on his uniform and assures the coach he understood what was taught to him. He remembers all the instructions. He will fail miserably, because he did not practice and do exercises to internalise them! Practice and exercise make knowledge an integral part of your nature such that, "When the rain descended, and the floods came, and the winds blew, and beat upon that house"— it was unshakable!

You are a product of what you know and a victim of your ignorance. Destruction in all forms comes because of a lack of knowledge. There is no difference between the spiritual and natural. In both, one requires solid knowledge to mount to a state of significance. Knowledge must be acquired and put into practice to achieve perfection. "Practice makes perfect" is true even in spiritual matters. Jesus said:

John 8:31. Then said Jesus to those Jews which believed on him, if ye continue in my word, then are ye my disciples indeed.

John 8:32. And ye shall know the truth, and the truth shall make you free.

The level of freedom you enjoy corresponds with your level of truth— knowledge. Your reality is governed by amount of knowledge you have.

Time Is Running Out

You may find life confusing. You thought you would figure it all out. But now, when you look back, you discover that time is running out. You are not yet settled. Your life is full of regrets and missed opportunities.

It doesn't have to be that way anymore. I have assisted thousands out of their predicaments! You can never solve a problem with knowledge from within the dimension that gave birth to the problem in the first place. You require knowledge from outside that dimension.

My life is a wonder. The knowledge and experience I have acquired over the last twenty-nine years have given me an enviable life. My family and children are desirable.

It starts with one honest acknowledgement that life could be better. Listen to the deep cries of your inner person, waiting to manifest. Each passing day is a wasted opportunity to start your journey into the best days of your life.

What are you waiting for? Time is not on your side. Take a step today and connect with me. Have you wondered how your life would have looked like if you knew exactly what to do at each one of those junctions where you were presented with multiple choices?

Most of the time you did not have solid knowledge. You guessed your way to your current position. You have an opportunity today to turn things around. I will help you discover the knowledge that will empower you to become the best you have always wanted to be. This is my speciality and my experience! Connect today and see your life transformed beyond recognition! It is not too late. Begin your journey today.

About Dr. Gerald Nyasulu

Prophet Gerald Nyasulu Ph.D., B.A (Public Administration) is an anointed and seasoned teacher of the Word of God who walks in signs and wonders. The level of prophetic revelation that you will receive under his ministry is mind blowing and life transforming. Countless people's lives have been totally transformed from mediocrity to greatness, from despair to clarity, from hopelessness to purpose driven!

111

Gerald's Offer

Give Prophet Gerald Nyasulu a chance to share his revelation and insights from the Scriptures to be the next on the line of testimonies. You don't have to continue living an average life because of lack of knowledge. Your greatest victory ever is probably just one revelation away! Enrol today and start your journey to greatness! This will be your best decision ever!

SchoolOfTheSpirit.com.au

Chapter 8: God is Greater Than Any Man! Your Faith Can Move Mountains | Collin Harrison

Has your life ever been turned upside down, in just a quick moment? When everything you knew to be normal, suddenly disappeared? It has happened many times for me, and I'm sure, for you, too. Life is fragile and unpredictable.

You can never know for sure what will happen next, but you should know about the value of resilience, hope, and the importance of cherishing every moment.

When I was a child, age 11, in Jamaica, my face and body began swelling up. My mother sent me to the doctor, in another district. I had to walk a long distance and sat in the waiting room, pondering what could have caused such a situation.

The swelling on my face did not look normal. The doctor looked at me and said, "It's not serious. It will disappear in a few days." He sent me back home with no medication. My mother was very concerned about the situation and took me back to the doctor the next day. My face was still very swollen.

The doctor tested my urine and wanted to send me directly to the hospital, which was 13 miles away directly, but my mother took me home to get some clothes. A car was hired by my family to take me to the Hospital which was in Port Maria, St. Mary. They admitted me, and I spent the next eight days in hospital.

During my Hospital stay, they gave me nine injections starting that night I was admitted, and continued injecting me for eight days as a patient. The local minister from my district, and one of the parishioners, visited with me, and prayed for me.

That was almost 60 years ago. I've never had another kidney problem since. I believe it was a miracle. Everyone I've known with kidney problems has either died or undergone dialysis treatment even up to date.

They can't be cured and must live with the condition for the rest of their lives, be it brief or extended.

But because those brothers prayed for me in the hospital, believing in God for healing, I have never had any more problems with my kidney. I am now in my 69th year, God be praised.

Understand God In A Wider Context

When I became a Christian at age 15, I gained understanding. I looked at Bible characters in terrible situations, who, instead of being bitter, gave thanks. I gave my own thanks, and continue to do so after experiencing my kidney issue. Understanding God in a wider context, I appreciated that if I had died, I wouldn't be here now. My sons wouldn't have been born. I wouldn't have had grandchildren. I wouldn't have met my wife of 43 years plus.

There's positivity in the fact that the experience happened to me, and that I can be an example to others. If you find yourself in a bad situation, don't lose hope. Don't lose faith, trust God through the process.

Though I did not understand it then, I now realise He is dependable.

You might fall into a "valley" where you can't see beyond the ridge. You might be thinking, "I'm on my last leg. What am I going to do?"

You don't have to suffer alone. You might think there's no hope. God works miracles every day. If he did it for me, he can do it for you.

Hear and feel connected. You may be going through this valid moment, but there is still breath in your body. There is still life, and when there is life, there is hope. You don't have to disappear.

Think positively. Tell yourself, "If I trust God, if it is His will, he will work it out, whatever the situation. If he works for my benefit, then I have reason to rejoice. If it doesn't work the way I would love it to work, I still give thanks, because I know He has something better planned.

Think positively. Trust God. Give thanks.

God Kept Us Safe In The Bus

In December 1979, my church family and I were travelling from Kingston to St. Catherine for a concert in the district of Darling Spring.

We always pray before one of those journeys. The evening before we departed, a worried young lady told me she could not join us. She was nervous about our event, because the last time she travelled, she suffered an accident and almost died— still bearing the scar of that accident.

As we boarded the bus, we prayed for God's guidance. We were happy and singing praises to God as we always do. We were less than a mile from our destination when the driver of the bus told us he was having difficulties, but our faith wasn't shaken because we believed that he was going to be able to take us safely, and we were trusting God.

We were going down a dangerous hill when he made this announcement, that the bus's brakes had failed. We were about to drive past a sharp curve. If he failed to negotiate the curve, we would end up into a river. We had no fear. The driver decided to try and "banked" the bus, sharply turning the steering wheel. The bus flipped, landed on a train track, and turned over. The bus was lying on its side, but we piled out without injuries.

A young lady in our group, who had a heart condition, had fallen asleep during the journey. She suffered no injuries and didn't know anything had happened until she woke up and the bus was already on its side. We believed that God had allowed her to sleep during this time so she would not be overly anxious or afraid.

Of all who were in the bus, over 40 of us— only one person had any injury, if one can call it that— she had a minor scratch. That's all!

God kept us safe in that bus. I don't have any other explanation. God sent and protected us so that we could attend our concert and sing praises to Him. We had a wonderful time at the concert that evening. We rejoiced because we had expected casualties or injuries from the bus accident. But instead, victory! What the Devil meant for evil, God meant for our good, as Joseph said to His brothers in Genesis 50:20, paraphrase.

I still believe in miracles. I still trust after all that has happened. God watches over us. We trust He will do whatever is necessary to help us out of a situation that otherwise would have been deadly. That would have decimated us or bring great suffering, He turned it into a testimony to encourage and strengthen others.

You have a destiny. Many of us temporarily walk outside of that destiny. God may still deliver for you in spite of you not walking your proper path. Jeremiah 29:11 says, "For I know the plans I have for you, plans to prosper you and not to harm you, plans to give you hope and a future." He knows everything about you. According to Psalm 139, He knew you before you were conceived in your mother's womb.

The omniscient God knows everything. He started the world. There's nothing He doesn't know about you. He knows when you are about to fail and what causes you to fail. He gives you leeway in the form of free will.

You are free to make the choice to walk in His path, or take our own path, to see where it leads. Sometimes He will nudge you right back into your path. Other times, he will lengthen the rope and let you go until you've come to the realisation that your path does not serve you. That's you suffering. Pain brings you back to Him, but sometimes, you miss those markers.

Trust In God

In 2001, my wife and I were about to be debt free with a paid-off mortgage. We were looking forward to buying a home in Jamaica to spend time between Britain and Jamaica in our retirement years.

My wife Esther had just turned 47 years old. She was the leader of our Sabbath school and one day, shortly after her birthday while leading the Sabbath school service, spoke to the brethren, by way of encouragement, saying, "I'm going to trust God. I will walk the way God wants me to walk. I will not be swayed by what others are doing or saying, I will be faithful to God's calling."

The following Thursday night she was speaking with her brother Lipton on the phone. The tenet of the conversation was the same as on the Sabbath— they encouraged each other to continue to see Jesus and Him only in spite of what was happening around them. She was fine, to the best of our knowledge. She was not overly concerned about anything as far as we were aware. She was a manager in one of our major Banks, where she had worked for over 30 years after leaving school. After speaking with her brother, we proceeded with our usual routine— we went to bed.

The following morning, which was Friday, I climbed out of the bed and into the bathroom, doing my morning routine. Usually, Esther would brush her teeth while I showered, but that day, she remained in bed. After my shower, I found her in bed and asked, "Esther, are you going to work today?" She replied, "Yes, but I feel so tired." She went to the bathroom, but rushed back into the bedroom almost immediately, and laid down on the bed.

At that moment, she suffered a stroke. She was unresponsive. I tried to gauge what was happening, but she was just looking at me, or so I thought. I called an ambulance, which arrived 15 minutes later. They took us to the emergency room where they tended her, and confirmed the prognosis of stroke. We were waiting for a bed until late in the evening, for a bed to become available on the stroke ward. She couldn't move, only looked. Esther could not do anything for herself.

She spent six months in the hospital, during which time she worked with a physio. The entire time, the church prayed in England, the USA, Canada, and the Caribbean islands. People who heard of the situation prayed for her.

It Is A Miracle

While she was in the hospital, I was there every day, morning until night, with her sisters, to wash her, and turn her in bed. She could not move.

About two months in, the consultant set up a meeting with myself, two other Doctors, the Matron, and one of my sisters-in-law in attendance. She laid out the case of my wife to us and at the end she said, "Mr. Harrison, we have done all we can do. Her situation will not improve. There won't be any change to what you are seeing."

I said to the consultant, "I don't believe that. I serve God. I believe she will walk and she will talk again.

And God has been faithful to His words. He said, "I will never leave you nor forsake you." — Hebrews 13:5.

Esther finally left the hospital in August. We had an appointment to return, to see the consultant again. When we got to her office, she had another appointment, so we waited outside until she was through. When she called for us, I asked Esther if she would like to walk into the office or use a chair? The consultant had heard the conversation.

Upon entering her office, the consultant told us, "The fact that you can offer her a choice of walking or sitting, is a miracle." She was amazed and had not expected that degree of recovery. She still has some difficulties walking distance, but I still believe she will do better than she is even now.

Esther still has difficulty speaking clearly, but she is understandable. Cognitively, she sometimes has trouble following a conversation if someone speaks too fast, but she is understanding and always happy.

When we visit the doctor, she asks, "Mrs. Harrison, how are you?" She always says, "Fine." She is always laughing. Yesterday, during a routine visit, our dentist said, "She's so happy. I wish all of my patients were like this," Remarking about the infectious laugh she takes everywhere she goes.

Esther brightens the day when we visit the doctor, physio, dentist, and eye specialist. One day, I asked her about her condition. "What can we do?" she answered, "We trust in God." I still believe that one day she will walk and talk properly.

Nothing Is Over Until God Says It Is Over

While there is life, there is hope, so don't despair. Keep trusting, keep as positive as you can be. Throughout your life, you will fall into deep situations where you can't help but think, "What is happening? Why am I in this situation?"

The solution: get back into a positive mindset. God has done so much for you. In the Bible, Job was going through a very hard time with those boils on his body that Satan caused. Job held onto his integrity and trust in God. His wife said to him, you're still holding onto your faith and trusting God after all of this.

Job said, "If I receive good, shouldn't I also receive evil?" Job 2:9-10. You can't expect to only receive "good." That's not the world we live in. Negative events happen.

The secret is to be in a mindset where you believe and trust in God, to survive the dark moments, and realise bad events are only a blip in the grand scheme of things. Manage stress, accidents, and tragedy, to the best of your ability. Trust Him, who is greater than all, to carry you through. Bad days will come, but they will also pass.

Cherish your loved ones. Never ever take one day for granted. Prioritise your health, safety, happiness, and sanity. Your own human resilience, support, compassion, and connection are valuable tools to overcome any obstacle and make the most of your life, no matter what challenges come your way.

I am Esther's carer and husband. Where I go, she goes, as is practical. But God always makes a way. I have made a pledge to her, that I will be with her to look after her, as long as we both shall live. Even if we only have one banana between us. And that's a pledge I intend to keep as long as I am able.

About Collin Harrison

Collin Harrison is a Jamaican author whose life experiences have led him to believe in the power of resilience, hope, and faith. He believes that even when life is unpredictable, God is greater than any man, and that faith can move mountains.

His personal experience of a miraculous healing from kidney problems led him to understand God in a wider context, and to appreciate the value of life and positivity. Collin believes in the power of prayer, and encourages you to trust God and think positively, no matter what life throws your way.

collin54harrison@gmail.com

Chapter 9: Dream Big And Take Massive Action | David Cavanagh

Like all good stories, this one starts, "Once Upon A Time..."

Once upon a time, there was a guy named David Cavanagh who had no money, was a single father of a beautiful daughter named Krystal, who was told by everyone how smart and awesome he was— yet, he could barely pay his rent each week.

So much for being "smart and awesome!"

David had to be the life of every party he attended. He was the "comedian and joker" everyone had to have around, but the "inside" of David was definitely not what he was portraying on the "outside." He was actually the joke of the party and not just the one telling the jokes.

David was a very lonely man who was crying out to be loved, to be wanted, to be noticed, to be listened to, and he did everything just to be the centre of attention.

This attention fed David's ego and low self-esteem to the level where it put a smile on his face. It kept him feeling "okay to be alive."

David was living in Mudgeeraba on the Gold Coast in Queensland, Australia, and his only form of income was receiving a single parent's pension each fortnight to help him, and his daughter Krystal, survive from day to day.

He was renting a three-bedroom townhouse with a guy named Dennis Hall and he could barely pay Dennis his half of the rent each week. Life was definitely not pleasant for David Cavanagh. In fact, it was living hell at the time.

"The" Phone Call

Then one day while David was at home laying on his couch, he got a phone call. The phone call was from Adam Hudson who was the co-founder of a company called the "Better Business Institute."

This company was run by Peter Sun and Adam Hudson— two very successful and talented marketers, entrepreneurs and businessmen who had kicked several home runs in many of their previous businesses.

Picture this: David was sitting at home and got Adam's phone call at 7:52PM in the evening when he was usually sitting down, relaxing, watching TV.

The phone conversation went something like this: "Hi David, it's Adam. Peter Sun and I are looking for someone to help with our in-house Internet Marketing and when we sat down and brainstormed, the name which kept coming into our heads was David Cavanagh. Do you mind coming in for an interview with Peter and I tomorrow morning?"

Of course, David said "Yes," and the following day, David went in to see Adam and Peter.

Now I'll recall everything as it happened looking back in hindsight:

When I was being interviewed back then, Adam told me how I was a really talented guy. He said I was an immensely talented guy when it came to copywriting, sales, motivation, personal development, persuasion, internet marketing, and SEO.

I felt so good when Adam complimented me because it filled my low self-esteem bucket and made me feel wanted, noticed, accepted, and loved at the time.

I thought, "I can't believe I'm hearing all these great comments about me." Then Adam dropped the bombshell on our great conversation:

"David, we feel you're focusing your energy 1% on 100 things, rather than putting 100% energy and focus onto one thing. If Peter and I are to employ you, you need to stop this immediately and start doing everything the way we ask you or you won't have a job."

This was the part of the conversation which really got up my nose.

Intense Focus

I didn't know whether to take Adam's comments as a huge insult, or to shut my mouth and put my pride and ego to the side and simply keep listening to him. I mean, what was I supposed to think at the time?

After all, he'd invited me in for an interview, so he must have felt I was definitely worth talking to in the first place. **Why was I doubting myself?**

Have you ever had the feeling of being down in the dumps, yet not knowing where to go or what to do with your life? That's what I felt like at that moment.

The feeling of not knowing who to turn to for help. The lack of thoughts of not knowing what direction you should be taking each and every day.

I was great at helping other people get massive results. This was me back then. This was a totally different David Cavanagh to the David Cavanagh nowadays. Now here are some huge takeaways for you:

I could have stayed the same. I could have kept talking rubbish to myself. I could have kept going on and on with the never-ending thoughts of how good I was, how I was better than everyone else, how I knew everything about anything (even though I was struggling to pay my bills, struggling to put food in my mouth each week, and the ongoing hassles of keeping the debt collectors away from my front door.)

I really needed to change my life, and Adam's words were the catalyst for me to start changing immediately. It was up to me to change. Change comes from within.

Follow One Course Until Successful

Three months after working with Adam and Peter, I was told by the team in the office how they were all flying down from the Gold Coast to Sydney to attend Tony Robbins' seminar called "Unleash the Power Within." I knew I had to be at this event. Something inside of me said, "Do whatever it takes to get to this event, David." Call it a "gut feeling," but I just knew I had to be there.

I asked Peter and Adam if they could pay for me in advance to attend the event, and I promised I'd pay them back out of my salary each week. It was putting myself into another "financial hassle" I didn't need, although my gut feeling told me I just had to do it.

I flew down to see Tony Robbins and made some totally crazy commitments to myself while I was there live at the event. I even wrote these commitments into the book I was given at the event and read them out to myself when I returned home to the Gold Coast.

"Get out of the relationship you're currently in... buy a brand-new car... stop focusing on helping everyone else and start looking after yourself for once in your life... leave Peter and Adam and speak on stages all around the world, teaching people how to make money online and offline."

Once I re-read everything I wrote, I thought I must have been delusional, and I wondered how in the world would I ever accomplish one of these far-fetched goals? (Let alone accomplish them all.)

Massive Action

I took massive action and made sure I put my heart and soul into achieving my goals and outcomes, which I wrote in my book. I knew I needed to do whatever it took at the time to "become the David I knew I could become" once I took and implemented everything with massive action.

Was it hard? Yes, it was extremely difficult. There were numerous times I felt like giving up, but giving up was what I'd always done, so it wasn't an option for me anymore. I'd given up, failed, and quit way too many times in the past, so it was time for change for the better. Have you ever done this before?

Am I glad I took massive action to achieve my goals and come out bigger and better on the other side? You better believe it! I'm extremely happy— it's made my life much better in so many ways. Ways in which I could never write about on paper.

Today, I'm married to Nisarat Cavanagh who is the best wife in the World for me. She treats me like a King, and I treat her like a Queen. We never argue or fight. We choose to understand each other and talk things through. To me, it's a marriage made in Heaven, and God sent me one of his Angels.

I'm blessed with a wonderful daughter Krystal who lives on the Gold Coast of Australia, and two beautiful daughters, Pannipa and Fahsai who live with Nisarat and I in Thailand. I have three daughters who I love very much (plus a grandson named Julius and a granddaughter named Annabella.)

Up until COVID time, I travelled the world teaching people how to make money online and offline. I've spoken at most of the World's biggest Internet seminars, workshops, and events as a keynote speaker. I've been voted Best Speaker at a lot of the seminars I've spoken at, which I'm very proud of.

I run 8, 10 and 12-day internet marketing workshops in Pattaya Beach, Thailand with Roger Bourdon and Bronwyn Mitchell (my coaching team) as well as my wife and business partner Nisarat Cavanagh with students flying in from all over the world to attend.

Who would have thought back then that David Cavanagh would change so much and be able to achieve all of these amazing results?

Moving Forward

You can achieve anything you want if you make a firm decision to do whatever it takes to achieve it. Think what you want, what you need to do, and then get out there and "just do it."

Secondly, you mustn't listen to people who bring you down in life. You mustn't listen to members of your family who tell you it can't be done. You need to start hanging out with people who truly care for you and your success and well-being.

Thirdly, you must take massive action and do everything within your power to achieve your goals, dreams, and outcomes. There are no "if's" and "but's."

Fourthly, never give up. If you need extra help, ask someone. If you need a push, join a mastermind group. Contact me for advice at David@DavidCavanagh.com if you're stuck in a rut and feeling bad about yourself.

You must learn to listen to the "inner you" which tells you that you can do and achieve anything in life if you make a decision, take action, and do whatever it takes until it's done.

Information without implementation is just "more information." Implement what you know needs to be done. The only truth is the end result. It's no good talking about what you're going to do. You need to get out there and do it right now. You need to start taking action immediately.

Get the results you truly deserve! Make yourself, your family, and friends proud of the "new you"— may your life from today onwards be your best life ever. I believe in you!

About David Cavanagh

David Cavanagh is an Internet Business Coach who travels the World giving keynote speeches to business owners about how to get more leads, conversions, sales, while obtaining the "number one position" in Google and YouTube.

David is a coach and mentor to the World's best leaders, helping business owners succeed in cosmetic surgery, law, travel, dental, SEO medical, legal marketing, real estate, and property development.

DavidCavanagh.com

Chapter 10: Reinvent Yourself And Act Fast | Pat Mesiti

I own a personally autographed book, *The Long Walk To Freedom*— the autobiography of Nelson Mandela. It is the story of a man who dared to have a vision for a new South Africa.

Mandela was the foster son of a Tembu chief. He grew up struggling with two worlds: the traditional culture of his tribe and the hostile reality of his white-dominated nation. His passion and vision grew out of the horrors and atrocities happening to his countrymen. Armed with fierce determination, he set a course to break down apartheid, and this led to a life in prison. But more than twenty years behind bars didn't stop his vision, and the world looked on in awe as this man made the progression from prison to presidency.

Vision & Reinvention

One of the imperatives for success in life is vision and reinvention. People who use vision, to reinvent themselves, achieve success.

Ray Kroc sold paper cups to restaurants in the 1920s and worked his way up to become a top salesman. But his vision went way beyond paper cups. He had a vision of making a big impact on the restaurant business, so he quit sales to market a machine that could mix several milkshakes at a time. **When you have a vision, opportunities come to you.** Through promoting the milkshake machines, he met the McDonald brothers, who ran a highly successful restaurant. They got talking and Ray Kroc ended up becoming their partner.

Driven by his vision, he came up with the concept of duplicating the McDonalds' restaurant on the other side of town. The two brothers opposed this, so Kroc bought the restaurant from them. Back at a time when hamburgers and chips were not an accepted meal, the pioneer began developing his empire. For the first eight years he poured all he had into the concept and saw few profits in return. But today it is a worldwide billion-dollar empire.

Ray Kroc had a vision, and he changed the world.

Walt Disney did the same. He approached 303 banks before he located one willing to finance his wild, crazy scheme to build a fun park with a cartoon mouse in a swamp area. Neil Armstrong, the first man to walk on the moon, said that ever since he was a boy, he'd had a vision of doing something important in aviation.

To be a successful person, regardless of your age, you must have a vision of where you want to be. Vision will cause you to be stretched far beyond the abilities you currently possess. It will launch you into abilities you don't have right now.

Will there be pain along the way? You bet. But betterment by its very nature is about vision, and being a better person is worth the pain it takes to get there.

An athlete has a vision for gold. A businessperson has a vision for success and profits. A mother has a vision for bringing up well-balanced children in a happy family. What is your vision for life?

Achievable, Challenging & Worthwhile Target

In the book *Vision, Values and Courage*, Neil Snider, James Dowd and Diane Morse-Houghton say: "Vision must provide a clear image of a desirable future. One that represents an achievable, challenging, and worthwhile long-range target."

Vision isn't a goal. It's a picture, a canvas on which you paint your future. It shows you what the future could and should look like. The businessperson's canvas shows them standing in front of a tall modern building with their company name on it— a sign of their success. The athlete's painting shows them standing on the dais holding up the gold medal, surrounded by cheering fans. And a young man wanting to win the heart of his sweetheart envisions himself at the altar with his beautiful bride.

Commitment to vision is an awesome power. If you decide to persistently move towards your vision over days, weeks, months, or even years, you will change your life, the lives of people around you, and your world. Regardless of setbacks.

Have you ever seen a successful athlete suffer injury and then come back to win the prize? A failed businessperson starting over again from zero to become a huge success? A husband and wife coming back from a failed marriage to build a solid, secure family unit? **These things happen because the vision stayed alive despite their circumstances.**

If you have a vision, it eases the pain when you face problems. They lose some of their sting. The vision lifts you above the difficulties and gives you strength to persevere through them and out the other side.

Once you are clear about your vision, you can reinvent yourself if your old self no longer serves you.

I have a friend who mastered the art of personal reinvention, but she wasn't always like that. She was bright at school, but her father was a military man — the family moved constantly. She dropped out of school in Year Ten, failing to adjust to a new school.

Before she got married, she did administration jobs. Then, she spent years at home looking after children. When her children were in primary school, she studied aged care and got a job in a nursing home. She studied social work, and before she'd completed her degree, secured a job working with the terminally ill. My friend loves this job. She gets to support and help individuals and their families at a daunting time. Now my friend is working full-time, caring for a family and doing a part-time course on helping the hearing impaired. She is inspirational. Can you reinvent yourself even when you're juggling family and work commitments? My friend says yes, and here is some advice from her on how to do it.

The Five Steps to Personal Reinvention & Ultimate Freedom

Be realistic. Sit down and count how many hours of work and learning you need to do, and whether this will fit around your home, life, and work duties. Be realistic when making this calculation. Manage your time well.

Plan ahead. You don't want to find yourself over committed and jeopardize both your existing career and personal life. To successfully reinvent yourself, you will need to carefully put a plan together. My friend recommends finding a quiet and comfortable place to work towards to learn or study where you won't be distracted or interrupted.

Schedule time for fun. You need time to work, rest and play. You will burn yourself out if you don't make time for friends, family, and leisure time (like walks on the beach and trips to the movies.) However, you need to come up with a schedule to balance work, learning new skills and family, and deliver on all fronts! But if your timetable is not working for you, be prepared to re-work it and shift items around. Consider leaving home an hour earlier a couple times a week and doing course reading in a coffee shop. Make it work for you, your team, and your family.

Ask for support when you need it. Don't try to be superman or superwoman. If you are finding the workload hard, ask friends or family for help. Friends may be your best form of support. Could anyone get some groceries or buy some frozen meals for you when you run out of time? Can you cut down your work hours? Can you hire help if you are overloaded?

The biggest advantage to continue working while you work towards reinventing yourself is that you still have an income coming in. Also, you are not stepping out of the workforce and damaging your career, and if the new skills you develop relate to your work, you are getting real-world experience. You can apply what you are learning to your current profession.

Working while learning new skills can be a win-win situation, but it can also be a lose-lose situation if you become exhausted and underperform at work and your new project.

Balancing work, learning, family, and leisure time is tricky. Some people will be able to manage it, others won't. Ask yourself how much you want it? What are you willing to sacrifice? What sort of support do you have around you?

Also, you ensure the timing is right. If reinventing yourself means the world to you, explore how you can make it happen. Start the process to reinvent yourself through further learning.

About Pat Mesiti

Pat Mesiti is a self-made multi-millionaire, gifted speaker, entrepreneur, mindset growth strategist, bestselling author, and consultant.

Pat' passion is to *equip* and *empower* you to experience growth and prosperity to your fullest potential. He *shifts mindsets* AND *builds bigger people* to produce results.

Free Audio: how to think like a millionaire and uncover the hidden fortune that lies within your mind:

Mesiti.com/freegift